GARDENER'S
DIARY

GARDENER'S DIARY

THE METROPOLITAN MUSEUM OF ART
NEW YORK

•

NEW YORK GRAPHIC SOCIETY BOOKS
LITTLE, BROWN AND COMPANY
BOSTON   LONDON   TORONTO

A NOTE ON THE ILLUSTRATIONS

The illustrations that appear throughout are adaptations of designs from *Les Fleurs et leurs applications décoratives*, a portfolio of works by the French artist and designer E. A. Seguy, published by the Librairie des Arts Décoratifs in Paris in 1901. Although very little is known about Seguy, he was active during the first third of the 20th century, producing a myriad of color portfolios containing designs that range from the floral motifs of Art Nouveau to the geometric stylizations of Art Deco. The portfolio plates were produced using the pochoir process, a hand-coloring stencil technique popular during the period. The portfolio is in the collection of the Department of Prints and Photographs of The Metropolitan Museum of Art. Purchase, Leon Lowenstein Foundation, Inc. Gift, 1976. 1976.581(1-30)

Copyright ©1988 by The Metropolitan Museum of Art

Published by The Metropolitan Museum of Art and
New York Graphic Society Books
New York Graphic Society Books are published by
Little, Brown and Company, Boston
Published simultaneously in Canada by Little, Brown & Company
(Canada) Limited

Produced by the Department of Special Publications,
The Metropolitan Museum of Art
Gardening consultant, Mary Ann McGourty
Designed by Miriam Berman
Photography by Walter J. F. Yee,
The Metropolitan Museum of Art Photograph Studio
Type set by Advance Graphic
Printed and bound in Italy by Sagdos S.p.A.

ISBN 0-87099-521-9 MMA
ISBN 0-8212-1701-1 NYGS (distributor)

CONTENTS

The monthly reminders
that appear throughout
"The Gardening Year"
are geared toward
moderate climates. If you
live in a very warm
or very cool area, please
adjust them accordingly.

THE GARDENING YEAR

○ Begin to plan spring flower beds, noting plants and seeds to be ordered.

○ Clean and repair gardening tools not attended to earlier.

○ Protect flower beds by covering them with branches cut from your Christmas tree.

○ See if you need more evergreens or ornamental grasses to add winter interest to your yard.

JANUARY

○ Keep bird feeders well stocked.

○ Review last year's garden notes and transfer important seasonal reminders into this year's diary.

○ Check houseplants frequently for mealybugs, mites, and other pests.

○ Root cuttings from overgrown houseplants.

JANUARY

○ Prune maples, birches, and dogwoods now, before sap begins to run.

○ Remove snow from evergreens by gently tapping the undersides of their branches with a broom.

○ Protect plants from damage by sprinkling sand, not salt, on slippery sidewalks.

○ Check for plant heaving during thaws and replace soil around roots.

JANUARY

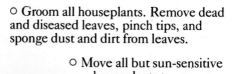

○ Groom all houseplants. Remove dead and diseased leaves, pinch tips, and sponge dust and dirt from leaves.

○ Move all but sun-sensitive houseplants to your brightest windows.

○ Begin to order seeds and garden supplies.

○ Begin to plan vegetable beds, remembering to rotate crops.

JANUARY

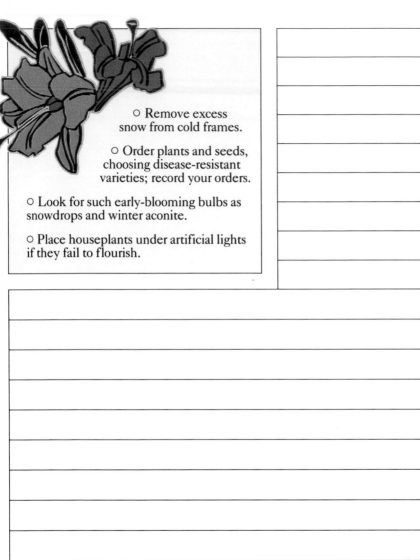

○ Remove excess snow from cold frames.

○ Order plants and seeds, choosing disease-resistant varieties; record your orders.

○ Look for such early-blooming bulbs as snowdrops and winter aconite.

○ Place houseplants under artificial lights if they fail to flourish.

FEBRUARY

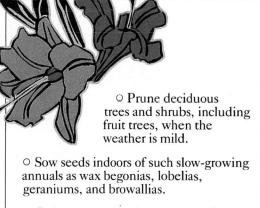

○ Prune deciduous trees and shrubs, including fruit trees, when the weather is mild.

○ Sow seeds indoors of such slow-growing annuals as wax begonias, lobelias, geraniums, and browallias.

○ Order peat pots and growing medium for starting seeds.

FEBRUARY

○ Check supplies
of insecticides and
fungicides, noting their
expiration dates.

○ Begin cutting branches of spring-
flowering shrubs for forcing.

○ Store seed packets in a cool, dry place
until needed.

FEBRUARY

○ Scrub pots and flats
needed for starting
seeds in spring.

○ Spray young evergreens
with an antidesiccant when
the temperature rises above 40° F.

○ Check stored bulbs, corms, and tubers
and discard any that have begun to rot.

FEBRUARY

○ Fertilize shade trees, evergreens, and ground covers.

○ Feed asparagus beds with lawn food.

○ Rotate crops to new positions as you lay out your vegetable garden.

○ Begin to remove winter mulch from flower beds.

MARCH

○ Remove damaged branches from trees and shrubs.

○ Continue to cut and force branches of spring-flowering trees and shrubs.

○ Sow seeds of such cold-tolerant vegetables as cauliflower, cabbage, and lettuce.

○ Avoid digging or stepping in wet flower beds.

MARCH

○ Sow seeds of tender vegetables and annuals indoors eight weeks before you expect the last frost.

○ Fertilize the lawn and treat it with a preemergent weed killer.

○ Transplant deciduous trees and shrubs while they are still dormant.

○ Keep seedlings started indoors cool at night.

MARCH

○ Cut ornamental grasses to the ground before new growth appears.

○ Prune summer-flowering vines and climbing roses.

○ Watch cold frames for rising temperatures and dryness.

○ Trim pot-bound houseplants and transfer to larger containers.

MARCH

○ Remove spent flowers from spring bulbs, but leave the foliage on until it dies back.

○ Plant such cool-weather crops as beets and broccoli.

○ Reseed bare spots in the lawn, then gently rake and water.

○ Remove tender tubers from storage.

APRIL

○ Soak bare-root plants in a very diluted fertilizer solution before planting.

○ Begin to move annual and vegetable seedlings to cold frames to harden them off.

○ Prune roses as new leaves appear.

○ Enrich soil with organic matter before planting.

APRIL

○ Treat fruit trees with dormant oil spray before they leaf out.

○ Prepare flower and vegetable beds as soon as the soil becomes dry enough to work.

○ Stake plants that will need support.

○ Thin or transplant seedlings when necessary.

APRIL

○ Divide established perennials when new growth reaches three to four inches.

○ Remove winter debris and remaining mulch from flower beds.

○ Install any necessary irrigation and drainage systems.

○ Rotate houseplants frequently.

APRIL

○ Apply any necessary weed controls to the lawn.

○ Control insects and diseases promptly to prevent severe infestations.

○ Remove extra suckers if they appear around raspberry bushes.

○ Remove spent flowers from such spring-flowering shrubs as lilacs.

MAY

○ Sow tender annuals and vegetables directly in the garden after the danger of frost has passed.

○ Apply summer mulch to garden beds to minimize weeding and watering.

○ Mow the lawn before the grass begins to mat.

○ Watch for weeds among ground covers.

MAY

○ Harden off seedlings and transplant to the garden after the danger of frost has passed.

○ Fertilize peonies and stake their stems to prevent rain damage.

○ Fertilize spring bulbs as soon as they finish flowering.

○ Prune vines after they finish flowering.

MAY

○ Plant such tender summer bulbs as gladiolus and dahlias.

○ Begin to move houseplants outdoors, protecting them from direct sun.

○ Replant ground covers where they have become sparse.

○ Divide and replant early-blooming perennials immediately after flowering.

MAY

○ Start next year's perennials and biennials from seed in the garden or in cold frames.

○ Treat roses and perennials regularly with fungicide to control mildew and black spot.

○ Loosen the roots of pot-bound nursery plants before planting them in the garden.

JUNE

○ Apply one inch of water to the soil each week if rainfall is inadequate.

○ Place nets over berry plants to guard them from birds.

○ Harden off any frost-tender seedlings that are still indoors.

○ Train cucumber plants and other vines on trellises.

JUNE

○ Root perennial
cuttings for next year.

○ Plant annuals in
bulb beds to hide
dying foliage.

○ Check rose plants for
Japanese beetles and set out
traps if necessary.

○ Pinch the tips of chrysanthemums
to promote compact growth.

JUNE

○ Clean and repair
the greenhouse for
next winter.

○ Separate clumps of
crowded spring bulbs,
but leave the foliage on
until it dies back.

○ Harvest early vegetables and
replant the garden with others
that flourish in the fall, such as
broccoli and Chinese cabbage.

JUNE

○ Place supports beneath melons to keep them off the ground and prevent rotting.

○ Note which plants are performing well and which are disappointing.

○ Dig up crowded bearded irises, divide them, and trim foliage back to six inches.

○ Keep houseplants away from air-conditioners.

○ Continue to spray fruit trees as needed.

JULY

○ Mist houseplants frequently.

○ Cut back excess growth on wisterias.

○ Cut flowers for drying when they are almost fully open, then hang them upside down in a cool place.

○ In hot weather, let the grass grow longer by raising the height of your lawn mower.

JULY

○ Check the lawn for grubs and larvae and treat if necessary.

○ Check for insects that thrive in summer heat and for hot-weather diseases, such as mildew.

○ Harvest broccoli before yellow flowers appear.

○ Stake tomato plants.

○ Check container plants frequently and water them freely when they become dry.

JULY

○ Protect seeds from strong summer sun by sowing them deeper than you did in the spring.

○ Prolong flowering by removing spent blossoms from plants.

○ Continue to water flower beds deeply if rain is scarce.

○ Continue to fertilize roses regularly.

○ Order bulbs for fall planting.

JULY

○ Make sure the greenhouse heating system is in good condition.

○ Water evergreens thoroughly to prepare them for fall and winter.

○ Plant more perennials for late summer and early autumn color.

AUGUST

○ Harvest herbs and dry them upside down in a cool place indoors.

○ Can or freeze fruits and vegetables as they ripen.

○ Continue to remove spent blossoms from plants and cut back unsightly foliage.

AUGUST

○ Fertilize roses at least six weeks before the first expected frost.

○ Order plants for fall.

○ Cut flowers during the coolest part of the day, either in the morning or the evening.

AUGUST

○ Water potted plants generously during hot weather.

○ Fumigate the greenhouse before moving plants inside for the winter.

○ Sow lettuce seeds in the garden for a fall crop.

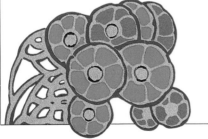

○ Discard all diseased and insect-damaged plants and foliage.

○ Dig up and pot herbs for kitchen use.

○ Reseed and fertilize lawns.

○ Protect tender vegetables from early frost.

SEPTEMBER

○ Take cuttings from begonias, geraniums, and other annuals for use as houseplants.

○ Prepare bird feeders for winter.

○ Check carefully for pests before bringing houseplants indoors.

○ Caulk and paint the cold frame.

SEPTEMBER

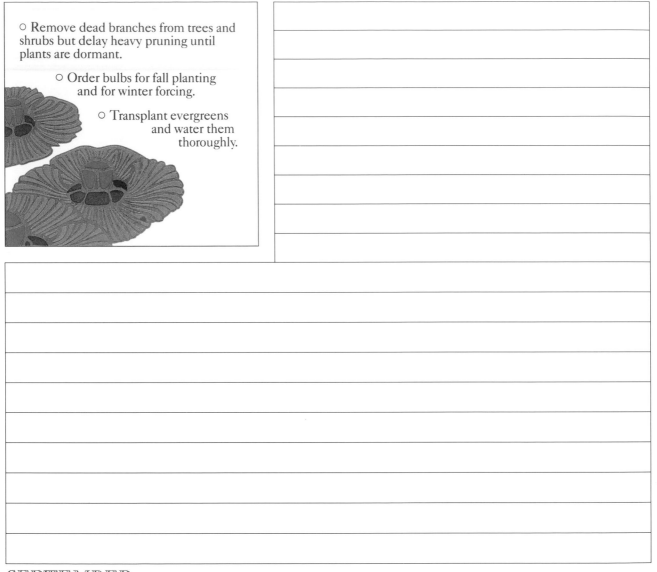

○ Remove dead branches from trees and shrubs but delay heavy pruning until plants are dormant.

○ Order bulbs for fall planting and for winter forcing.

○ Transplant evergreens and water them thoroughly.

SEPTEMBER

- ○ Begin garden cleanup, adding leaves and clippings to the compost pile.

- ○ Dig up tender bulbs, dry them in the sun, then store them for winter.

- ○ Divide and transplant perennials after they finish flowering.

SEPTEMBER

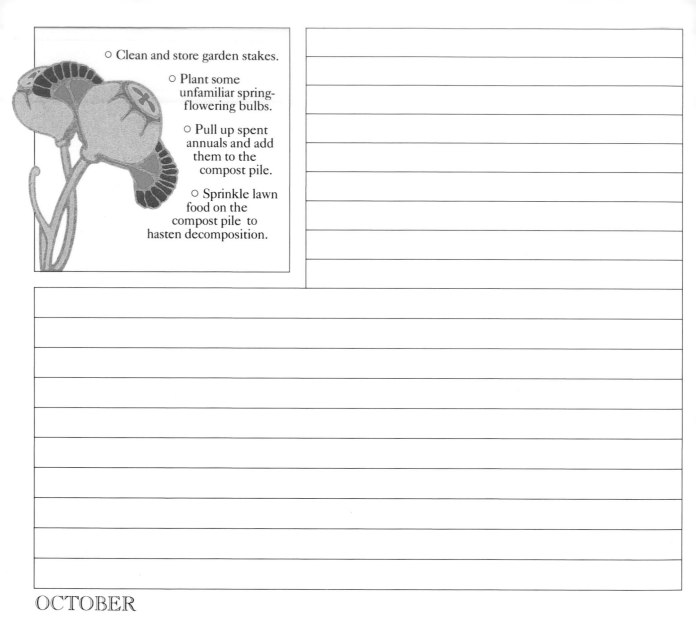

○ Clean and store garden stakes.

○ Plant some unfamiliar spring-flowering bulbs.

○ Pull up spent annuals and add them to the compost pile.

○ Sprinkle lawn food on the compost pile to hasten decomposition.

OCTOBER

○ Plant deciduous trees and shrubs after leaves have fallen.

○ Pick tomatoes, apples, and other fruits if frost threatens, and put them in a cool, dark place to ripen.

○ Continue mowing the lawn as long as the grass is growing.

OCTOBER

○ Dig up tender perennials and place them in cold frames.

○ Harvest winter squash and pumpkins with their stems attached to prevent rot.

○ Pot paper-white narcissus and other bulbs to force for late-winter blooming indoors.

OCTOBER

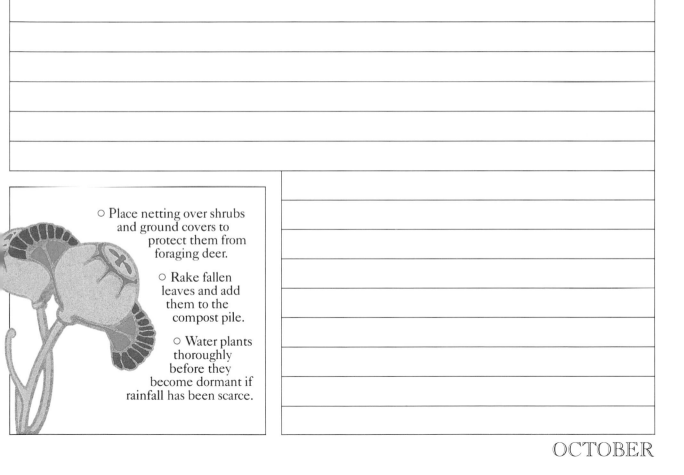

○ Place netting over shrubs and ground covers to protect them from foraging deer.

○ Rake fallen leaves and add them to the compost pile.

○ Water plants thoroughly before they become dormant if rainfall has been scarce.

OCTOBER

○ Add any necessary organic matter and lime to the soil for next year's garden.

○ Begin to collect evergreen boughs for winter mulch; apply them after the ground freezes.

○ Use burlap windbreaks to protect recently planted evergreens from exposure.

○ Continue weeding until the ground freezes.

NOVEMBER

○ Water cold frames thoroughly and add rodent bait before closing them down.

○ Note new plants to try growing next year.

○ Set out bird feeders and fill them.

○ Dig up all remaining root vegetables and store them carefully or mulch them heavily with hay.

NOVEMBER

○ Turn off outdoor water taps and drain them.

○ Prevent wind damage by fastening vines securely to supports.

○ Clean out the vegetable garden and flower beds, adding disease-free material to the compost pile.

NOVEMBER

○ Mow wildflower meadows.

○ Leave ornamental grasses standing for winter interest.

○ Cut perennials back before the first snowfall.

○ Turn the compost pile after the first hard frost to eliminate rodents.

○ Drain and store all hoses.

NOVEMBER

○ Plan spring deck, patio, and porch plantings.

○ Bring the bulbs you are forcing into the sun for holiday bloom.

○ Watch sun patterns to see if broadleaf evergreens are becoming scorched.

○ Place winter mulch on garden beds after the ground has frozen.

DECEMBER

○ Watch for falling temperatures in the greenhouse.

○ Apply antidesiccants to newly planted evergreens when the temperature rises above 40° F.

○ Set tree guards around fruit trees to prevent rodent damage.

○ Evaluate the year's outstanding successes and its biggest disappointments.

DECEMBER

○ Gather pine cones and cut greens for holiday decorations.

○ Avoid overwatering houseplants.

○ Water freshly cut Christmas trees every day.

○ Increase humidity around all houseplants.

○ Clean, repair, and sharpen gardening tools.

DECEMBER

PLANNING THE GARDEN

GARDEN DESIGN

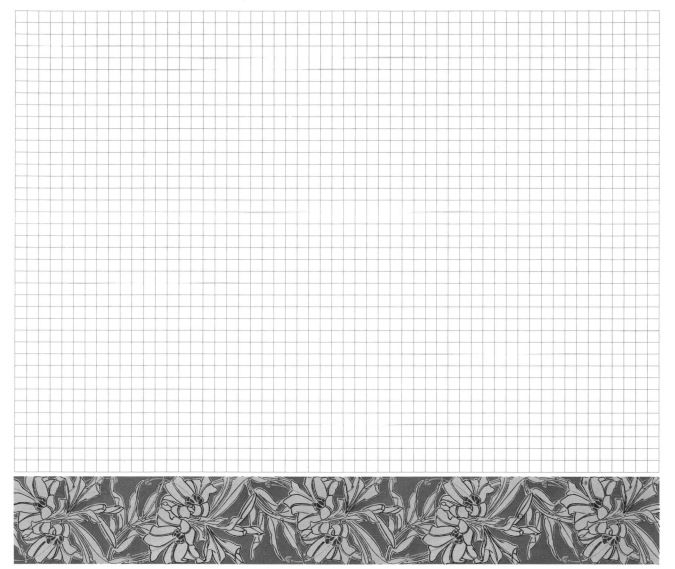

GARDEN DESIGN

GARDEN DESIGN

GARDEN DESIGN

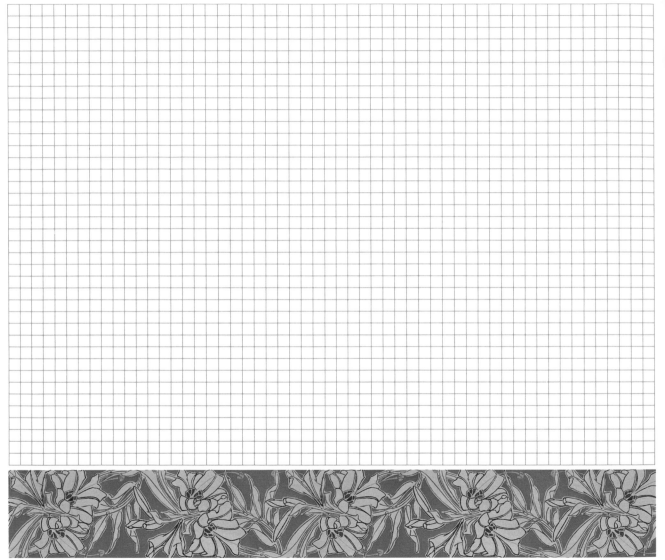

GARDEN DESIGN

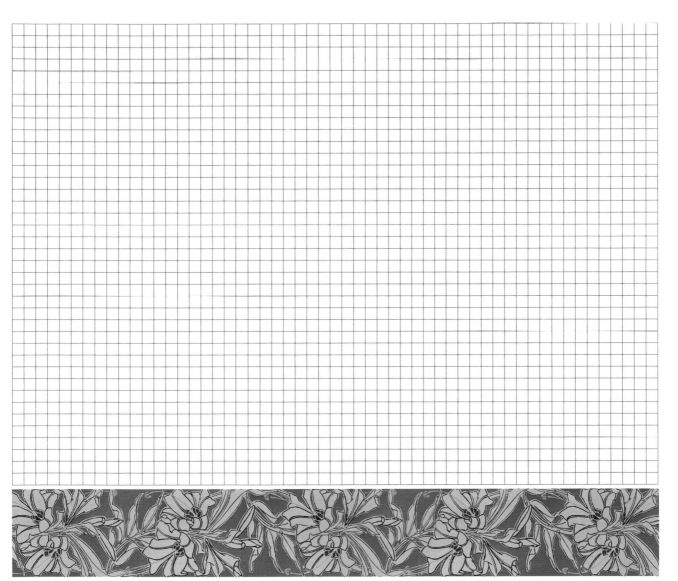

GARDEN DESIGN

GARDEN DESIGN

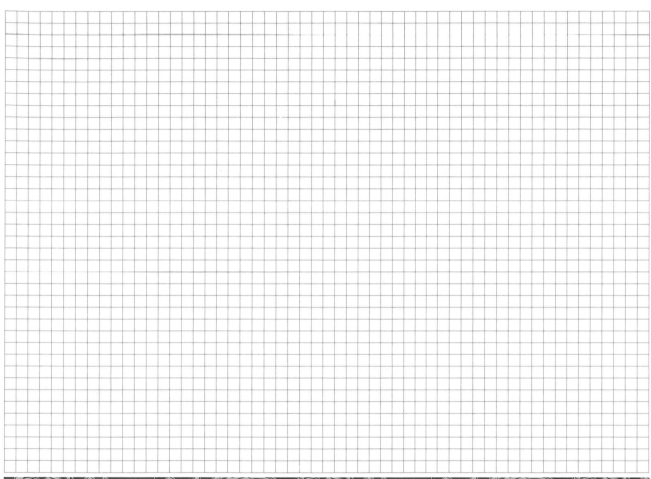

GARDEN DESIGN

PLANT	LOCATION	COLOR, HEIGHT & FLOWERING TIME

NEW PLANTS TO GROW

PLANT	LOCATION	COLOR, HEIGHT & FLOWERING TIME

NEW PLANTS TO GROW

PLANT	LOCATION	COLOR, HEIGHT & FLOWERING TIME

NEW PLANTS TO GROW

PLANT	LOCATION	COLOR, HEIGHT & FLOWERING TIME

NEW PLANTS TO GROW

PLANT	LOCATION	COLOR, HEIGHT & FLOWERING TIME

NEW PLANTS TO GROW

PLANT	LOCATION	COLOR, HEIGHT & FLOWERING TIME
_____	_____	_____
_____	_____	_____
_____	_____	_____
_____	_____	_____
_____	_____	_____
_____	_____	_____
_____	_____	_____
_____	_____	_____
_____	_____	_____

NEW PLANTS TO GROW

PLANT	DATE BEGUN	FLOWERING OR HARVESTING DATE

PLANTING SCHEDULE

PLANT	DATE BEGUN	FLOWERING OR HARVESTING DATE

PLANTING SCHEDULE

PLANT	DATE BEGUN	FLOWERING OR HARVESTING DATE

PLANTING SCHEDULE

PLANT	DATE BEGUN	FLOWERING OR HARVESTING DATE

PLANTING SCHEDULE

PLANT	DATE BEGUN	FLOWERING OR HARVESTING DATE

PLANTING SCHEDULE

PLANT	DATE BEGUN	FLOWERING OR HARVESTING DATE

PLANTING SCHEDULE

PLANT	DATE BEGUN	FLOWERING OR HARVESTING DATE

PLANTING SCHEDULE

RECORD
KEEPING

ITEM	ORDERED & RECEIVED	SUPPLIER	QUANTITY & COST

TOOLS AND SUPPLIES ORDERED

ITEM	ORDERED & RECEIVED	SUPPLIER	QUANTITY & COST

TOOLS AND SUPPLIES ORDERED

ITEM	ORDERED & RECEIVED	SUPPLIER	QUANTITY & COST

TOOLS AND SUPPLIES ORDERED

ITEM	ORDERED & RECEIVED	SUPPLIER	QUANTITY & COST

TOOLS AND SUPPLIES ORDERED

PLANT	DATE STARTED	DATE ROOTED OR GERMINATED	DATE MOVED OUTDOORS

PROPAGATION RECORD

PLANT	DATE STARTED	DATE ROOTED OR GERMINATED	DATE MOVED OUTDOORS

PROPAGATION RECORD

PLANT	DATE STARTED	DATE ROOTED OR GERMINATED	DATE MOVED OUTDOORS

PROPAGATION RECORD

PLANT	DATE STARTED	DATE ROOTED OR GERMINATED	DATE MOVED OUTDOORS

PROPAGATION RECORD

PLANT	DATE STARTED	DATE ROOTED OR GERMINATED	DATE MOVED OUTDOORS

PROPAGATION RECORD

PLANT	DATE STARTED	DATE ROOTED OR GERMINATED	DATE MOVED OUTDOORS

PROPAGATION RECORD

PLANT	DATE STARTED	DATE ROOTED OR GERMINATED	DATE MOVED OUTDOORS

PROPAGATION RECORD

PLANT	DATE STARTED	DATE ROOTED OR GERMINATED	DATE MOVED OUTDOORS

PROPAGATION RECORD

ITEM	ORDERED & RECEIVED	SUPPLIER	QUANTITY & COST

PLANTS, SEEDS, AND BULBS ORDERED

ITEM	ORDERED & RECEIVED	SUPPLIER	QUANTITY & COST

PLANTS, SEEDS, AND BULBS ORDERED

ITEM	ORDERED & RECEIVED	SUPPLIER	QUANTITY & COST

PLANTS, SEEDS, AND BULBS ORDERED

ITEM	ORDERED & RECEIVED	SUPPLIER	QUANTITY & COST

PLANTS, SEEDS, AND BULBS ORDERED

ITEM	ORDERED & RECEIVED	SUPPLIER	QUANTITY & COST

PLANTS, SEEDS, AND BULBS ORDERED

ITEM	ORDERED & RECEIVED	SUPPLIER	QUANTITY & COST

PLANTS, SEEDS, AND BULBS ORDERED

ITEM	ORDERED & RECEIVED	SUPPLIER	QUANTITY & COST

PLANTS, SEEDS, AND BULBS ORDERED

ITEM	ORDERED & RECEIVED	SUPPLIER	QUANTITY & COST

PLANTS, SEEDS, AND BULBS ORDERED

ITEM	ORDERED & RECEIVED	SUPPLIER	QUANTITY & COST

PLANTS, SEEDS, AND BULBS ORDERED

ITEM	ORDERED & RECEIVED	SUPPLIER	QUANTITY & COST

PLANTS, SEEDS, AND BULBS ORDERED

COMPANY	SERVICE RENDERED & COST	COMMENTS

NURSERY AND LAWN SERVICE CONTRACTS

COMPANY	SERVICE RENDERED & COST	COMMENTS

NURSERY AND LAWN SERVICE CONTRACTS

PLANT	DATE PLANTED	DURATION OF FLOWERING	COMMENTS

FLOWER RECORD

PLANT	DATE PLANTED	DURATION OF FLOWERING	COMMENTS

FLOWER RECORD

PLANT	DATE PLANTED	DURATION OF FLOWERING	COMMENTS

FLOWER RECORD

PLANT	DATE PLANTED	DURATION OF FLOWERING	COMMENTS

FLOWER RECORD

PLANT	DATE PLANTED	DURATION OF FLOWERING	COMMENTS

FLOWER RECORD

PLANT	DATE PLANTED	DURATION OF FLOWERING	COMMENTS

FLOWER RECORD

PLANT	DATE PLANTED	DATES HARVESTED	COMMENTS
_____	_____	_____	_____
_____	_____	_____	_____
_____	_____	_____	_____
_____	_____	_____	_____
_____	_____	_____	_____
_____	_____	_____	_____
_____	_____	_____	_____
_____	_____	_____	_____
_____	_____	_____	_____

VEGETABLE RECORD

PLANT	DATE PLANTED	DATES HARVESTED	COMMENTS

VEGETABLE RECORD

PLANT	DATE PLANTED	DATES HARVESTED	COMMENTS

VEGETABLE RECORD

PLANT	DATE PLANTED	DATES HARVESTED	COMMENTS

VEGETABLE RECORD

PLANT	DATE PLANTED	DATES HARVESTED	COMMENTS

VEGETABLE RECORD

PLANT	DATE PLANTED	DATES HARVESTED	COMMENTS

VEGETABLE RECORD

PLANT	DATE PLANTED	COMMENTS

THE HERB GARDEN

PLANT	DATE PLANTED	COMMENTS

THE HERB GARDEN

PLANT	DATE PLANTED	COMMENTS

THE HERB GARDEN

PLANT	DATE PLANTED	COMMENTS

THE HERB GARDEN

PLANT	DATE PLANTED	COMMENTS

TREES, SHRUBS, AND VINES

PLANT	DATE PLANTED	COMMENTS
_____	_____	_____
_____	_____	_____
_____	_____	_____
_____	_____	_____
_____	_____	_____
_____	_____	_____
_____	_____	_____
_____	_____	_____
_____	_____	_____

TREES, SHRUBS, AND VINES

PLANT	DATE PLANTED	COMMENTS

TREES, SHRUBS, AND VINES

PESTS AND
DISEASES

PROBLEM	DATE	REMEDY & RESULTS
_____	_____	_____
_____	_____	_____
_____	_____	_____
_____	_____	_____
_____	_____	_____
_____	_____	_____
_____	_____	_____
_____	_____	_____
_____	_____	_____

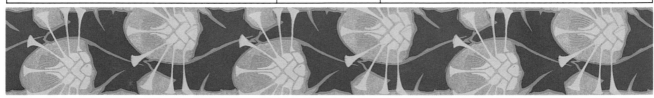

PESTS AND DISEASES

PROBLEM	DATE	REMEDY & RESULTS

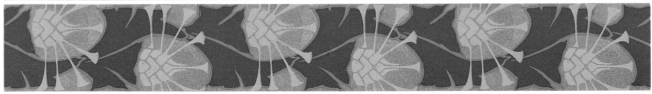

PESTS AND DISEASES

PROBLEM	DATE	REMEDY & RESULTS

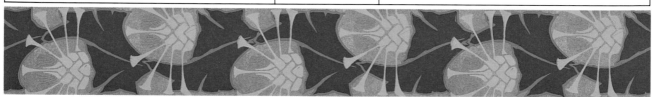

PESTS AND DISEASES

PROBLEM	DATE	REMEDY & RESULTS

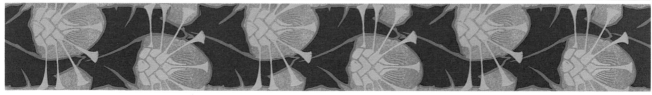

PESTS AND DISEASES

PROBLEM	DATE	REMEDY & RESULTS

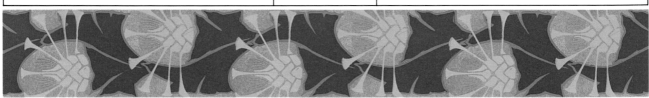

PESTS AND DISEASES

SOIL IMPROVEMENTS

DATE OF SOIL SAMPLE	PH LEVEL	RECOMMENDED IMPROVEMENTS	IMPROVEMENTS MADE
_____	_____	_____	_____
_____	_____	_____	_____
_____	_____	_____	_____
_____	_____	_____	_____
_____	_____	_____	_____
_____	_____	_____	_____
_____	_____	_____	_____
_____	_____	_____	_____
_____	_____	_____	_____

SOIL ANALYSIS

TYPE & BRAND	DATE APPLIED	LOCATION	RESULTS

FERTILIZERS

TYPE & BRAND	DATE APPLIED	LOCATION	RESULTS

FERTILIZERS

TYPE & BRAND	DATE APPLIED	LOCATION	RESULTS

FERTILIZERS

TYPE & BRAND	DATE APPLIED	LOCATION	RESULTS

FERTILIZERS

NURSERIES
AND
GARDENS
VISITED

NAME & LOCATION	DATE	PLANTS OF NOTE

NURSERIES AND GARDENS VISITED

NAME & LOCATION	DATE	PLANTS OF NOTE

NURSERIES AND GARDENS VISITED

NAME & LOCATION	DATE	PLANTS OF NOTE
————————————————	————————	———————————————————
————————————————	————————	———————————————————
————————————————	————————	———————————————————
————————————————	————————	———————————————————
————————————————	————————	———————————————————
————————————————	————————	———————————————————
————————————————	————————	———————————————————
————————————————	————————	———————————————————
————————————————	————————	———————————————————

NURSERIES AND GARDENS VISITED

NAME & LOCATION	DATE	PLANTS OF NOTE

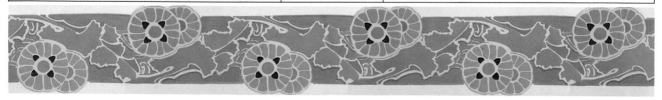

NURSERIES AND GARDENS VISITED

NAME & LOCATION	DATE	PLANTS OF NOTE

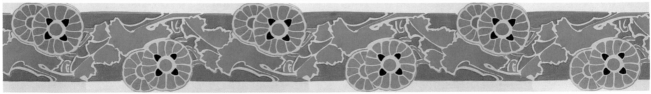

NURSERIES AND GARDENS VISITED

CLUBS AND MAGAZINES

CLUB OR MAGAZINE	YEARLY DUES OR SUBSCRIPTION FEE	DATE PAID

CLUBS AND MAGAZINES

CLUB OR MAGAZINE	YEARLY DUES OR SUBSCRIPTION FEE	DATE PAID

CLUBS AND MAGAZINES

CLUB OR MAGAZINE	YEARLY DUES OR SUBSCRIPTION FEE	DATE PAID

CLUBS AND MAGAZINES

CLUB OR MAGAZINE	YEARLY DUES OR SUBSCRIPTION FEE	DATE PAID

CLUBS AND MAGAZINES

CLUB OR MAGAZINE	YEARLY DUES OR SUBSCRIPTION FEE	DATE PAID

CLUBS AND MAGAZINES

GARDENING
BOOKS

TITLE	AUTHOR	COMMENTS

GARDENING BOOKS

TITLE	AUTHOR	COMMENTS

GARDENING BOOKS

TITLE	AUTHOR	COMMENTS

GARDENING BOOKS

TITLE	AUTHOR	COMMENTS

GARDENING BOOKS

TITLE	AUTHOR	COMMENTS

GARDENING BOOKS

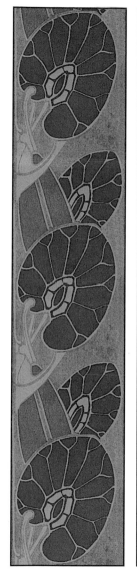

SUPPLIERS

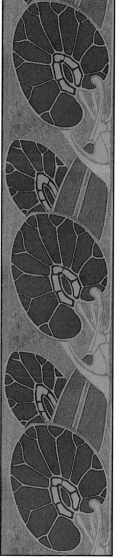

NAME

ADDRESS

TELEPHONE

SPECIALTY

NAME

ADDRESS

TELEPHONE

SPECIALTY

NAME

ADDRESS

TELEPHONE

SPECIALTY

NAME

ADDRESS

TELEPHONE

SPECIALTY

NAME

ADDRESS

TELEPHONE

SPECIALTY

NAME

ADDRESS

TELEPHONE

SPECIALTY

SUPPLIERS

NAME

ADDRESS

TELEPHONE

SPECIALTY

NAME

ADDRESS

TELEPHONE

SPECIALTY

NAME

ADDRESS

TELEPHONE

SPECIALTY

NAME

ADDRESS

TELEPHONE

SPECIALTY

NAME

ADDRESS

TELEPHONE

SPECIALTY

NAME

ADDRESS

TELEPHONE

SPECIALTY

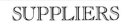

SUPPLIERS

NAME

ADDRESS

TELEPHONE

SPECIALTY

NAME

ADDRESS

TELEPHONE

SPECIALTY

NAME

ADDRESS

TELEPHONE

SPECIALTY

NAME

ADDRESS

TELEPHONE

SPECIALTY

NAME

ADDRESS

TELEPHONE

SPECIALTY

NAME

ADDRESS

TELEPHONE

SPECIALTY

SUPPLIERS

NAME

ADDRESS

                                                    TELEPHONE

SPECIALTY

NAME

ADDRESS

                                                    TELEPHONE

SPECIALTY

NAME

ADDRESS

                                                    TELEPHONE

SPECIALTY

NAME

ADDRESS

                                                    TELEPHONE

SPECIALTY

NAME

ADDRESS

                                                    TELEPHONE

SPECIALTY

NAME

ADDRESS

                                                    TELEPHONE

SPECIALTY

SUPPLIERS

NAME

ADDRESS

                                TELEPHONE

SPECIALTY

NAME

ADDRESS

                                TELEPHONE

SPECIALTY

NAME

ADDRESS

                                TELEPHONE

SPECIALTY

NAME

ADDRESS

                                TELEPHONE

SPECIALTY

NAME

ADDRESS

                                TELEPHONE

SPECIALTY

NAME

ADDRESS

                                TELEPHONE

SPECIALTY

SUPPLIERS

NAME _____

ADDRESS _____

_____ TELEPHONE

SPECIALTY _____

NAME _____

ADDRESS _____

_____ TELEPHONE

SPECIALTY _____

NAME _____

ADDRESS _____

_____ TELEPHONE

SPECIALTY _____

NAME _____

ADDRESS _____

_____ TELEPHONE

SPECIALTY _____

NAME _____

ADDRESS _____

_____ TELEPHONE

SPECIALTY _____

NAME _____

ADDRESS _____

_____ TELEPHONE

SPECIALTY _____

SUPPLIERS

NAME

ADDRESS

TELEPHONE

SPECIALTY

NAME

ADDRESS

TELEPHONE

SPECIALTY

NAME

ADDRESS

TELEPHONE

SPECIALTY

NAME

ADDRESS

TELEPHONE

SPECIALTY

NAME

ADDRESS

TELEPHONE

SPECIALTY

NAME

ADDRESS

TELEPHONE

SPECIALTY

SUPPLIERS

PHOTO
RECORD

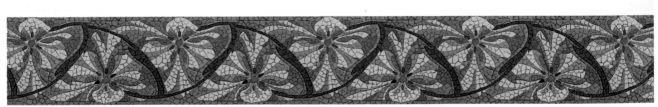

PHOTO RECORD

PHOTO RECORD

PHOTO RECORD

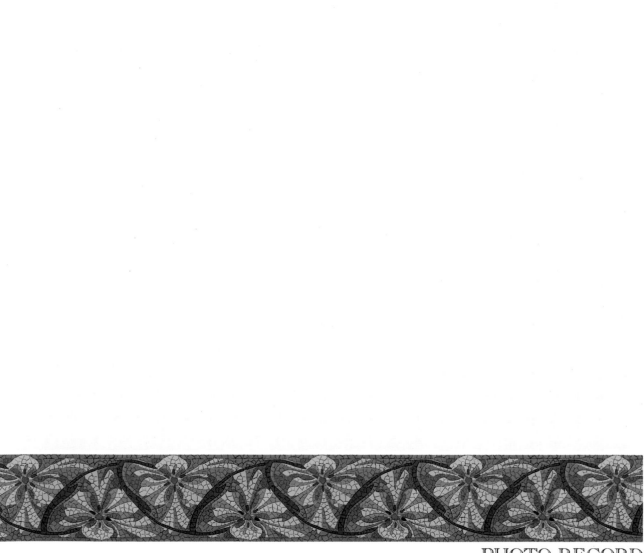

PHOTO RECORD

PHOTO RECORD

PHOTO RECORD

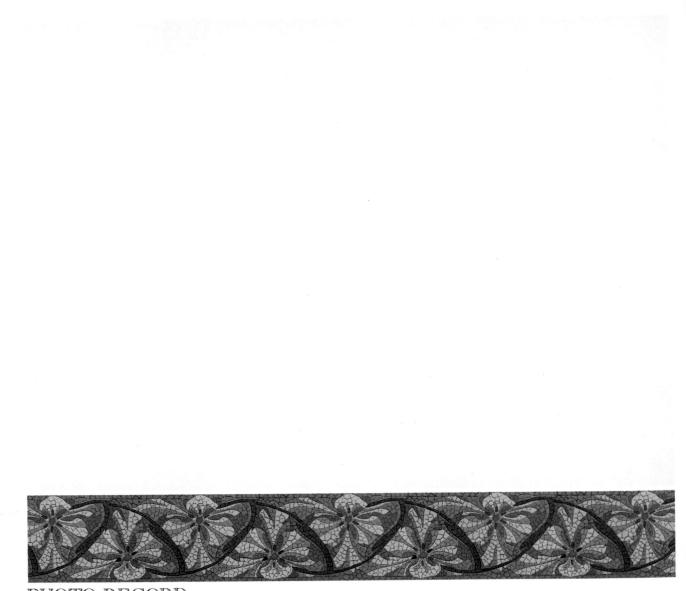

PHOTO RECORD

PHOTO RECORD

PHOTO RECORD